Physical Science

MATTER

by Abbie Dunne

CAPSTONE PRESS

a capstone imprint

Pebble Plus is published by Capstone Press,
1710 Roe Crest Drive, North Mankato, Minnesota 56003
www.mycapstone.com

Library of Congress Cataloging-in-Publication Data
Names: Dunne, Abbie, author.
Title: Matter / by Abbie Dunne.
Description: North Mankato, Minnesota : Capstone Press, [2017] | Series:
    Pebble plus. Physical science | Audience: Ages 4-8. | Audience: K to
    grade 3. | Includes bibliographical references and index.
Identifiers: LCCN 2016005333| ISBN 9781515709398 (library binding) | ISBN
    9781515709718 (pbk.) | ISBN 9781515711063 (ebook (pdf))
Subjects: LCSH: Matter—Juvenile literature. | Matter—Properties—Juvenile
    literature.
Classification: LCC QC173.16 .D86 2017 | DDC 530.4—dc23
LC record available at http://lccn.loc.gov/2016005333

Editorial Credits

Linda Staniford, editor; Veronica Scott, designer; Eric Gohl, media researcher;
Katy LaVigne, production specialist

Photo Credits

Capstone Studio: Karon Dubke, 13; Shutterstock: Africa Studio, 17, Andrey Armyagov, 20 (bottom), Ilike, 11, Lori Sparkia, 19, mavo, cover, Pigprox, 15, studiots, 5, Tnymand, 9, vitalez, 7, Yevhen Tarnavskyi, 20 (top)

Design Elements: Shutterstock

Note to Parents and Teachers

The Physical Science set supports national curriculum standards for science. This book introduces the concept of matter. The images support early readers in understanding the text. The repetition of words and phrases helps early readers in understanding the text. This book also introduces early readers to subject-specific vocabulary words, which are defined in the Glossary section. Early readers may need assistance to read some words and to use the Table of Contents, Glossary, Read More, Internet Sites, Critical Thinking Using the Common Core, and Index sections of the book.

Printed in the United States of America.
082017   010708R

Table of Contents

What is Matter?

Everything in the world
is matter. Matter is anything
that takes up space.
Your bed and books are matter.
You are made of matter.

States of Matter

Matter can be a solid, liquid, or gas. Trees, rocks, and buildings are solid. Rivers and lakes are liquid. The air is a gas.

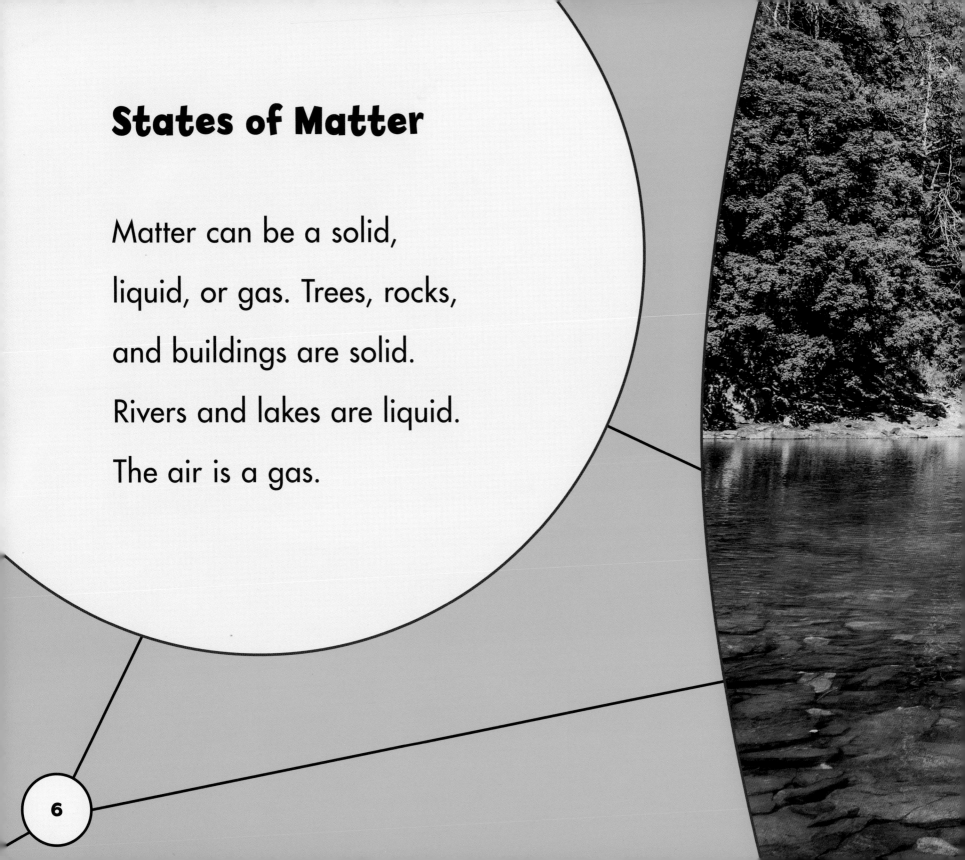

Solids

Solids keep their shape and size.

Some solids are hard.

They don't bend easily.

Rocks, ice cubes, and metal

are hard solids.

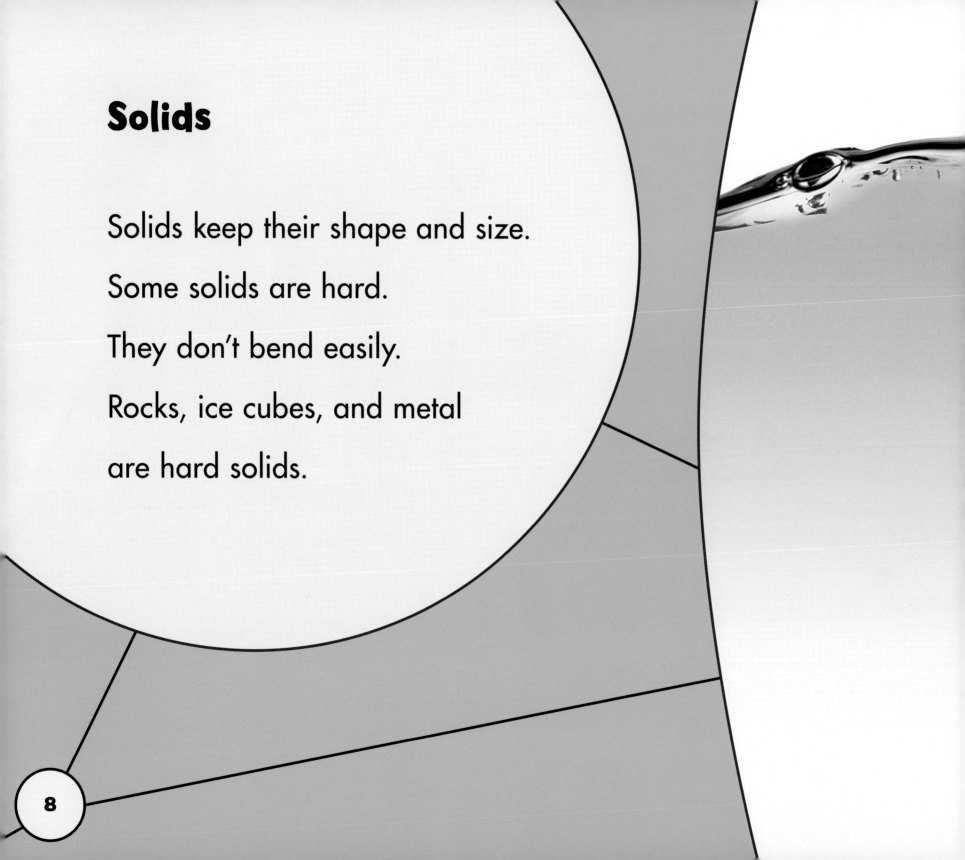

ice cubes
are solid

Some solids change shape easily.
You can form modeling clay
into different shapes.
Rope can be twisted into a knot.
Tree branches can bend.

Liquids

Liquids do not have their own shape. A liquid takes the shape of the container that holds it. Milk, water, and shampoo are liquids.

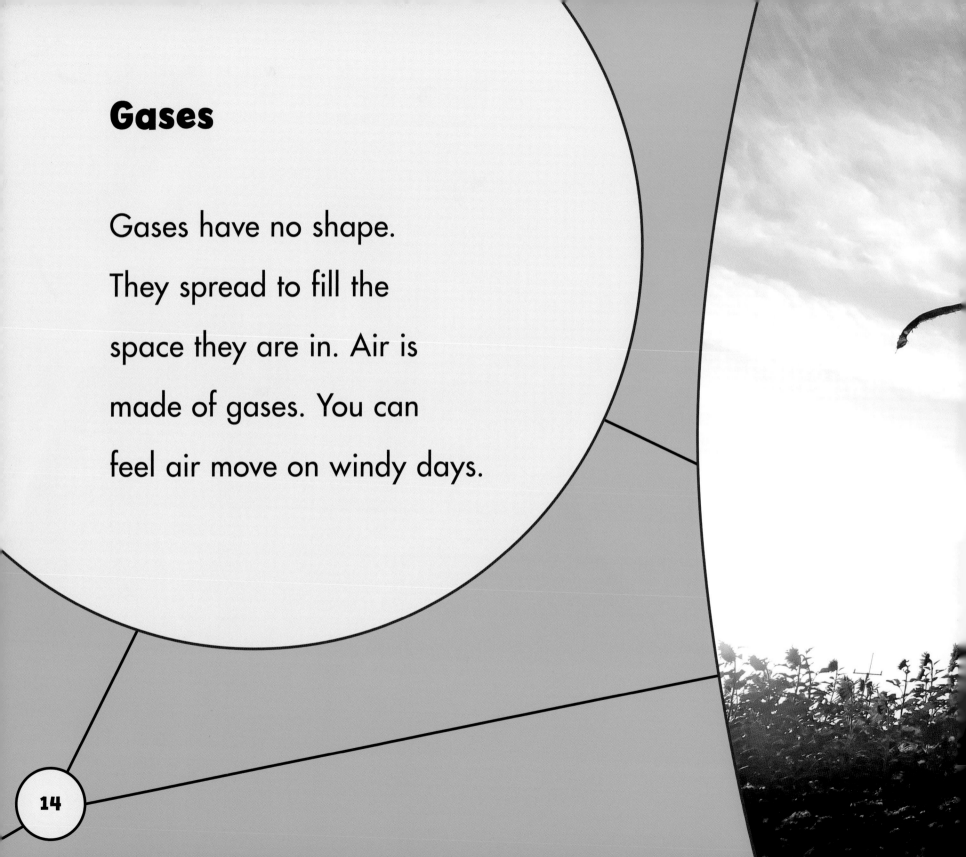

Gases

Gases have no shape. They spread to fill the space they are in. Air is made of gases. You can feel air move on windy days.

Mixing Solids and Liquids

Some solids and liquids can be mixed together. Paint changes the color of water. Salt dissolves in water. You can tell it is there if you drink the water.

Changing Matter

Matter can change forms.
Ice cream melts on a hot day.
Water turns to ice in the
freezing cold. Boiling water
turns to steam.

Activity

Predict how a solid might change when it is put into water. Then do the following experiment to find out.

What You Need

- permanent marker
- 2 sandwich-size self-sealing bags
- water
- ice cube
- antacid tablet
- camera or crayons and paper

What You Do

1. Write "ice cube" on one bag. Write "antacid tablet" on the other bag.

2. Fill each bag half full of water.

3. Zip each bag almost closed until there is just enough room to squeeze in an ice cube or the antacid tablet.

4. Put the ice cube in the bag marked "ice cube". Squeeze the rest of the air out of it and zip it closed.

5. Put the antacid tablet in the bag marked "antacid tablet". Squeeze the rest of the air out of it and zip it closed.

6. Use the camera to record what you see, or make a drawing of what happened.

What Do You Think?

Make a claim. A claim is something you believe to be true.

How do some solids change when placed in water?
Use the results of your experiment to support your claim.

Glossary

dissolve—to disappear into something else

gas—something that is not solid or liquid and does not have a definite shape

liquid—matter that is wet and can be poured, such as water

matter—anything that has weight and takes up space

solid—a substance that holds its shape

Read More

Oxlade, Chris. *Experiments with Matter and Materials.* Excellent Science Experiments. New York: PowerKids Press, 2015.

Rompella, Natalie. *Experiments in Material and Matter with Toys and Everyday Stuff.* Fun Science. North Mankato, Minn.: Capstone Press, 2016.

Troupe, Thomas Kingsley. *Why Do Dead Fish Float?: Learning About Matter with the Garbage Gang.* The Garbage Gang's Super Science Questions. North Mankato, Minn: Capstone Press, 2015.

Internet Sites

FactHound offers a safe, fun way to find Internet sites related to this book. All of the sites on FactHound have been researched by our staff.

Here's all you do:

Visit *www.facthound.com*

Type in this code: 9781515709398

Check out projects, games and lots more at **www.capstonekids.com**

23

Critical Thinking Using the Common Core

1. When water freezes, which state of matter does it become? (Key Ideas and Details)

2. Explain some features of matter that is liquid. (Craft and Structure)

3. Liquids take the shape of the container they are in. What do you think happens when a liquid is spilled? (Integration of Knowledge and Ideas)

Index